for
My Forever
Circle

by
Maure Quilter

Azalea Art Press
Sonoma . California

ISBN: 978-1-943471-75-1

Cover Photos by:
Cyndi Dresser

In Memoriam
Maure Quilter

July 18, 1936 —
January 7, 2024

Preface

Maure once told me she'd written in her head since she was five years old. I imagine she continues to compose letters, newsletters, and stories for her *Forever Circle* as she watches and prays over us all. As she once wrote about the end of life, "…this moment is not an ending but a graceful pivot into eternal life."

When I met Maure twenty years ago at one of my first writing work-shops, I had no idea it was the beginning of a relationship that would span two decades.

She called me her writing teacher, but the truth was much greater than that.

She believed in me and when she believed in someone, her loyalty was boundless. I imagine you can relate.

When she faced a divorce in her late 70's, she called to request private writing sessions. We began a week later, and she continued until March 2023, when, due to memory loss, writing was no longer a pleasure for her. It was heartbreaking for us both when our writing ritual came to an end.

Our meetings always began with an inspirational quote or image, followed by two minutes of silence and a writing prompt to spark her muse. Maure enthusiastically put pen to paper, wrote for about 20 minutes, and then read her piece aloud. We both marveled that in all those years, there were only two times she labored to find her writing voice.

Maure always inspired me with her wisdom, inspiration, and love of self-reflection. When she began to lose her eyesight in 2019, she wasn't ready to suspend her writing practice, so I transcribed her words while she 'wrote on air.'

The quotes shared in this book are gleaned from those writings. A huge debt of gratitude goes to Karen Mireau for reading through Maure's pieces and capturing her essence with such perfection.

Maure's spirit lives on through the countless selfless acts of kindness she offered and the many insights and wisdom that flowed so generously from her open heart and onto the page.

I hope this humble sampling of her writings provides you comfort as you grieve the loss of a beloved friend, therapist, spiritual companion, or family member.

With Love,
Mary Tuchscherer
January 2024

"We're all just
walking each other home."

— *Ram Dass*

It's taken me a long, long time to stop and think about what my own truth is.

Looking from my perch on
my 87-year-old mountain
and trying to figure out
how I arrived here,
I realize once again how all
experiences grow us into
who we become in old age.

What a mystery!

I am rich beyond measure
with resources and blessings.

I see the blue sky, the green
grass, a few blossoming trees
and as always, I am deeply
grateful and simply must
keep on keeping on
with love.

I can't imagine
how I became so blessed
from years and years ago
to be bathed in peace
and protected by loved ones
as well as angels and saints —
so precious to me.

I do believe some of us are
exceptionally blessed to be
on this planet and see the
Earth's infinite possibilities.

I realize these gifts, freely
given, and I protect them
as I go about my day.

The word 'walk' speaks
volumes. Walking our life
home and sharing this
individual and unique
journey is our mandate.

We are called into life
not alone but into the family
of human kind. Like it or not
we are never alone.

We must walk home
whether we like it or not.

I can imagine some of us
swinging hands, skipping
into our tomorrows
or on days burdened
with pain, distress or worry.

We lean onto and into each
other's energy. Walking
implies pushing ourselves
along no matter the burden
of inertia that might sit on us,
so that no matter what the
day asks of us or the night
burdens us with we continue.

I believe in miracles
and self-challenges.

We can take little steps,
bless those steps and have a
good word for those we love
and even those whose beliefs
sometimes annoy
and challenge us.

So, we must try to do
what we can as best we can
day in and day out.

I feel it is important, even
essential, to look in my own
mirror and be with me.

I somehow really enjoy the
phrase 'be with' concerning
myself. It is simply a gentle
statement of how I feel
when I take time to write
and reflect.

That simple phrase
keeps me growing
into my growing self.

I don't think many people
realize how important it is to
be with our very own selves,
taking time to listen, observe,
and even appreciate
how we mysteriously
and amazingly evolve.

We may never know
where our blessings go
or how kindness affects
even a stranger,
but no matter.

Whatever we share
contributes
to the greater good.

I think it's up to women
to create and design new
ways to live justice for all.

I've always thought that
but now I can see many more
dimensions, especially
racially, sexually, age wise,
and for those of us living
with our disabilities.

It is not easy and we never
know what may befall us.

I send comfort, peace
and courage to all of us
carrying burdens, to all of
our loved ones who are
struggling for the right and
good, and asking that we be
inspired toward good will,
kindness and whatever we
need to live an honorable life
of truth and decency.

What a mystery we are to
ourselves and each other!

The amazing thing to me is
that I feel this truth
in my very bones.

I realize my life has never
been mine and mine alone
to live.

Every breath I take or choice
I make effects everyone
nearby whether they know it
or not.

I love the word comfort,
it's my cat's name.

I love the word and the
experience and it's pretty rare
for me to feel it. I long for it.

I don't think I've had that
much comfort in my life
along with the losses
I've had.

I think that's too sad because
I am good at comforting.

It's one of my gifts that
with or without words
I can comfort.

Looking back on my life
I think I have been a source
of comfort for friends
who have responded to me.

We may often observe
those we admire evolving
and admire their diverse and
mysterious ways they grow,
but I don't think we reflect
enough on our own evolving.

It is a beautiful mystery
and the outcomes are gifts
we return to ourselves.

Sacred friends might also
reflect back to us our
mysterious evolution
and that is special.

Friends may see dimensions
of ourselves we haven't
noticed and that, too,
is quite a gift.

If we believe our friends,
trust them for their truths,
then we have something to
carry with ourselves the next
times, months, days, weeks
we live.

I want to be loving
and peaceful.
I want harmony
and blessings
that keep me whole.

I want to love my friends and
I want the next phase of my
life to bless me and others in
some way that might surprise
me or bless all of us
in some way.

I hope to continue to create
and love and grow and create
something I haven't done
before.

Amazingly,
I can even meet
a newish self
that I have not realized
before.

Isn't that something?

Here I am, 86
or should I say 86 ½.
I see myself in a new way
even after all these many
miles I have walked. In a way
it is always new to me,
my new steps, my new
journey, and even my new
hours and moments
I've been given to live.

Imagine that!

If I were my own best friend,
I would tell myself to always
remember to relax about life,
relax about all things.

It tickles me because I think
others might say that
about me.

I accept this journey without
judgment or criticism.
I try to accept the messages
that come to me
whether they come with
capital letters or in a
mysterious code.

That acceptance is never easy
but it is what I have done
as I try to figure out my
whole life.

Pushing 87,
my whole life
is no small thing.

Tenderness is one of my
favorite ways to feel.
Tenderness calls me to a
hidden secret way
to be in life.

A tender awareness may
sneak up on me
and undo me to myself.
Sometimes the feelings
evoked by another undo me.

The feelings bubble up
and surround me before I
even realize it.

Those moments of
tenderness I treasure.

I appreciate the gifts
the days bring me
and I usually find them.

It's the little gifts that bless
us and carry us along.

It is amazing that we are each
given one and only one life
that at least I know of
and we do not know the
length of that life or the
challenges of our particular
trip on this planet.

But it is ours to fulfill
and complete whatever that
may be. Isn't that a mystery?

We don't know how long it
will be or how we may write
our own story but it is our
and ours alone to share.

There is much I want to
understand, to accept
and possibly to share as long
as I continue to live.

While I cannot believe
I've lived this long,
it seems to be the plan.

I ask God
and all the angels and saints
to open my eyes to all the
greater good given to me
while I am here, and ask that
I recognize this greater good
every minute of every day.

It is my hope
that I find each day's gifts,
see them and bless them as I
accept and honor each
blessing.

I am grateful for all my hundreds of companions who have joined me in my lifetime, gifted me in ways I never realized, lifted me, carried me, energized me.

Love evolves
and stretches us
in so many ways.

I learn so much
from all those who have
touched my life
and broadened me
along the way.

I am grateful to have been
loved, to have loved, and to
nourish that grace quietly
and blessedly in its
mysterious way.

Love is all
and is in all for us
to sip often
and savor . . . always.

Photo of Comfy
by Cyndi Dresser

A special thank you to
Colleen Hendricks and family.

With gratitude for all those
who contributed to this book,
for those present with Maure
during her last days,
and for the many friends,
if unnamed here, who loved
and continue to love her.

Cyndi Dresser

<u>Maure's
Garden Group:</u>

Carol Gegner
Kathy Jones
Connie Kinney
Mary Lowen
Charlotte Wolter

Colleen Hendricks

Jordan Hendricks

Megan and Cindy
at Ivy Park Walnut Creek
Assisted Living

Barbara McDaniel

Karen Mireau

Keith Schroeder

Madonna Treadway

Mary Tuchscherer

Walnut Creek
Threshold Choir

To contact the publisher
please email
Azalea.Art.Press@gmail.com

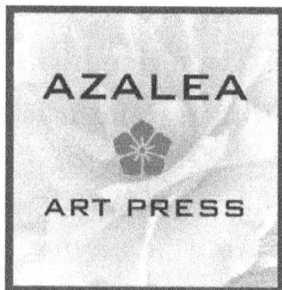

To order this book
please visit
www.Lulu.com

www.ingramcontent.com/pod-product-compliance
Lightning Source LLC
Chambersburg PA
CBHW031336040426
42443CB00005B/363